Psychological Storms:
The African American
Struggle for Identity

Thomas A. Parham, Ph.D.

African American Images
Chicago, Illinois

DEDICATION

To my wife Davida, older daughter Tonya, my mother Sadie, Pam, Billy and Gerald, and extended family for their unwavering support and love. This one is for you, Dad.

To Kenya, my youngest daughter, in the hope that her discoveries of color differences and her battles with oppression will never compel her to deny her cultural authenticity as a jewel from Mother Africa.

To Reverend John Nix McReynolds, the Pastor of Second Baptist in Santa Ana, California, for creatively blending the principles and practices of Christianity in service to African people.

To God and the Ancient Ancestors in hopes that my words and deeds will reflect Your way and You will be pleased.

ACKNOWLEDGEMENTS

Thanks to Ms. Peggi Cummings, my administrative assistant, for the extensive hours spent in typing this manuscript and preparing it for press.

To Brother Tyrone Howard, a research assistant, for his contributions to the investigative phases of this project.

To Dr. Wade Nobles for his critical review and insights and his contribution in writing the introduction.

To Dr. Aldrich Patterson for his helpful suggestions.

To Drs. Joseph White, Janet Helms and Horace Mitchell, my mentors, for their guidance and support throughout my professional development.

To Drs. Na'im Akbar and Wade Nobles for helping to educate me in the ways of our people.

To Brother Adisa Ajamu for his Afterword.

TABLE OF CONTENTS

TABLE OF CONTENTS

CONTINUED

◆

PREFACE

My formal education as a psychologist began in 1977 when I entered graduate school. By Western standards, it culminated with my receiving my Doctor of Philosophy degree (Ph.D. in Psychology) in 1982. During those five years, I had to demonstrate considerable competence, among other things, in the areas of: understanding general personality and specific counseling theories, testing and assessment, research design and statistics, psychopathology, career development, life span development, and principles and practice of individual and group counseling and psychotherapy techniques. With all this wealth of knowledge; however, I was ill equipped to provide an accurate conceptual analysis of my condition as an African American male in America. I also learned through my own initiatives, life experiences, and by listening to the reservoirs of wisdom in our community, the elders.

While I was fortunate enough to emerge from my educational experiences relatively unscathed, I recognized both at a rational and intuitive level that something other than my personal mastery of the principles and practices of Eurocentric psychology was the guiding force behind my achieving that milestone. Undoubtedly, the keys to my success were a strong belief in and identification with God the Creator, a supportive biological and extended family network, my affiliations with the National Association of Black Psychologists (ABPsi), the Association for Multicultural Counseling and Development (AMCD), the Minority Fellowship Program in the American Psychological Association, and the personal and literary mentorship I received from strong African American writers, scholars and friends.

Within this context, I owe a special extension of gratitude to Joseph L. White, Janet Helms, Horace Mitchell, Robert L. Williams, Rod McDavis, Halford Fairchild, Oliver Slaughter, Robert Guthrie, Thomas Gunnings, Bobby Wright, William Cross, Linda James Myers, Reginald Jones, Wade Nobles, Na'im Akbar, Harriet and John McAdoo, A.J. and Nancy Boyd-Franklyn, James Jones, Jawanza Kunjufu, Clement Vontress, Asa Hilliard, W.E.B. DuBois, Francis Cress-Welsing, Haki Madhubuti, Cheikh Anta Diop, George James, Molefi Asanti, Maulana Karenga, Malcolm X, Carter G. Woodson, Marcus Garvey, Frederick Douglas, James Baldwin, Frantz Fanon, Ivan Van Sertima, and many others too numerous to name. Indeed, their influence has been profound, penetrating and lasting.

Their collective influence on my personal and intellectual growth and maturity as a psychologist and author has helped me to recognize that my own contributions to African people must be the continual struggle for psychological, physical, and spiritual liberation. However, liberation first and foremost requires that African Americans must

II

come to the realization that White racism and a program of White supremacy is alive, well, and thriving in the nineties. Racism is both an unconscious recognition of the anxiety many Whites feel in relation to people of color, as well as a manifestation of White people's need to compensate for their own insecurity or perceived inferiority through the use of power, control (intellectual, spiritual, and military), and domination of African people (Cress-Welsing, 1991; Bradley, 1981). These efforts of control and domination make perfect sense if one understands that the principles and practices of oppression are primarily psychological in nature. Thus, the control over physical space (geography), modes of production (labor), and the educational and religious indoctrination of a people all involve a reformation of the psyche of the oppressed victim. The consequence is the deliberate construction of the psychologically rooted political, economic, social, educational, and religious systems which are designed to guarantee the survival of the White race and place them (Whites) at the center of the world. Also, given the Eurocentric propensity for dichotomous thinking (either/or) and a belief in a "difference equals deficiency" logic, African Americans have been and may always be on the negative end of any conceptual analysis provided by Europeans, regardless as to whether the polarities represent good-bad, best-worse, or superior-inferior.

My observation is not intended to indict every person who is White. In my heart, I believe that the hard core racists are a small percentage of the White population. I do believe, however, that there are not enough White anti-racists who are willing to confront other Whites who display such insensitivities. The issues of race and racism are so anxiety provoking for most Whites that they appear to do whatever is necessary to avoid even discussing it. Isn't it interesting that even when Whites do create a forum for discussing racism in America (literature, television, radio, etc.), most analyses of the issues focus on the oppressed rather than the oppressor. Consequently, White people rarely (if ever) confront their own racist attitudes and feelings nor analyze the dynamics of their own behaviors toward people of color.

If we assume that this evasive posture on the part of Whites will continue, the prospect of making wholesale systemic change in the institutions of America is less than optimistic. This observation is critical because I believe that too many African Americans look to White society and White people and their institutions in order to feel good about themselves. The tendency to seek approval and validation from your oppressor is psychologically maladaptive because feeling good about yourself is impossible if your referent is based on the perceptions, feelings, and attitudes of a people who hold you and your entire race in contempt.

Indeed, if change is going to come it must come from within, from within ourselves and from within our communities. African people in America, and throughout the diaspora for that matter, can no longer afford to wait on White people, White communities, and White institutions to empower us. We must empower ourselves. To do so, however, requires an awareness and insight into our psyche which allows us to get in touch with those parts of us that have been damaged by 400 years of oppression in this country.

Given this state of affairs, it is incumbent upon every African American to place his or her own African cultural perspective at the center of any analysis or conceptual schema involving people of African descent. Accordingly, the struggle for psychological liberation in particular requires a recognition of who the oppressor is, how systems of oppression impact our individual and collective psyche, and a commitment to change any cognitive, emotional, or behavioral fibre of our being which does not support, affirm, and enhance our humanity as African people. This work is presented in the hope that it will in some small way contribute to that effort.

Thomas A. Parham, Ph.D.

INTRODUCTION

"It's up to the living to keep in
touch with the dead, Eli.
Man's power doesn't end with death.
We just move on to a new place, a place where we
watch over our living family...
The ancestors and the womb...they're
one, they're the same.
Those in the grave, like those who're
across the sea, they're with us.
They're all the same.
The ancestors and the womb are one.
Call on your ancestors,
Eli. Let them guide you.
You need their strength.
Eli, I need you to make the family strong again, like
we used to be.
Call on those old Africans,
Eli. They'll come to you when you
least expect them.
They'll hug you up quick and soft
like the warm sweet wind.
Let those old souls come into your heart, Eli.
Let them feed your head with wisdom that ain't from
this day and time."

Nana Peasant, from
"Daughters of the Dust" *by Julie Dash*

It is clear to me that many of the African centered Black Psychologists have been "hugged up quick and soft and fed with wisdom" by those old Africans and Dr. Parham is amongst the best who are being lifted up by the ancestral spirit and given the charge to realign our tongues with our hearts.

Thomas Parham's *Psychological Storms: The African American Struggle for Identity* is a new yet old genre of African psychological analyses and critique. The genre of the allegorical tale or story is found at the roots of African psychological thought. As early as the writing of "The Eloquent Peasant" (Circa, 1800 BCE), African thinkers have used the allegorical tale to reveal "below the surface thinking" and deep hidden processes that are not readily revealed in simplistic observation or analyses. Like "The Eloquent Peasant" where the ancestors pointed out, through dialogue/discourse, the correct moral character or nature of African people while calling attention to the social devastation resulting from our moving away from our own traditions, values, customs and beliefs, Dr. Parham is calling our attention to the psychological consequences of being forced away from our way.

Dr. Parham's obedience to the African cultural precept (law) of "consubstantiation" allowed or compelled him to "see" the meaning of this feature of the African cultural substance and its social application in the African proverb that states, "what is true above, so too shall it be true below." Accordingly, Dr. Parham skillfully points out both the true character of African American people and the devastation resulting from the reformation of our psyche due to being victimized by racism and colonialization.

"Those old souls" (intelligences) allowed and accurately directed Dr. Parham to "see" that the same spirit or essence that defines the complexities of divinely governed natural atmospheric phenomena (i.e., hurricanes) also defines the intricacies of divinely governed human psychological development (i.e., personality/identity). Parham notes in this regard that the clash of high pressure systems with low pressure systems is analogous to the clash of African and European cultural worldviews. If the "Eye of the Storm" is that place of calmness in the center of destructive energy, then the need to "(re)center" oneself in ones own authentic cultural essence is instinctually understood as the place where African Americans can balance the pressures stemming from the constant and continuous assault on our humanity.

Dr. Parham invokes both our ancestral and modern understanding of "the storm" and, in so doing, he has reintroduced the self to ourselves with the mirror of traditional wisdom and technique. Parham points out that the biogenetic cultural makeup of the personality creates for each individual a set of needs which must be satisfied. He further suggests that the cultural distinctiveness of African people colors the very nature (essence) of what the human need is, as well as, what is necessary to satisfy the need at any given moment. In reading *Psychological Storms: The African American Struggle for Identity*, the reader cannot dismiss the haunting realization that the identity of the African American is rooted deeply in the sense of Africanness or Africanity and that the sense of Africanity is a critical feature in successfully responding, adapting and mastering the challenges of human degradation targeted at Africans by a White Supremacist society.

In utilizing the insights gained from a divinely governed natural universe, Parham guides the reader to watch more closely the laws governing "the forming of the storm" as "below the surface thinking" regarding African American responses to White authority, racist/oppressive government leadership as well as our social movements and interpersonal relations.

In centering his analyses in the (re)emerging African centered epistemology and paradigm, Parham critiques the full force of the storm as parallel to the psychological storms experienced in the African American community. He notes, in this regard, that destruction is predictable because it is lawful. The reversal of the destruction (i.e., healing) must likewise be lawful. In noting that the African centered personality theorists (e.g., Akbar, Azibo, Baldwin, Myers, etc.) have suggested that "the core of Black people's identity is essentially African in nature and partly biogentically determined," Parham systematically points out that while every aspect (i.e., thoughts, feelings and behavior) of the psychic destruction experienced by African Americans is found in the wake of the destructive path of the storm, the reversal or rehabilitation process (healing) will, however, require the use of developmental laws that are congruent with the nature and essence of

African people and not those of the storm.

Dr. Parham's *Psychological Storms: The African American Struggle for Identity* recognizes the essential consequence of our psychological storm and notes that the degree of psychological and even behavioral devastation experienced by African Americans will correspond directly to the degree that one includes Eurocentric values into ones life. With the astuteness of a scientist and the insights of a mystic, ergo Imhotep, Dr. Parham provides a clear and useful critique of the psychological methods for managing the discomfort and dysfunctions resulting from the Hurricane. This alone is a needed contribution to the field.

In writing *Psychological Storms: The African American Struggle for Identity* Dr. Parham has, without a doubt, let "those old souls" feed his "head with wisdom that ain't from this day and time."

Wade W. Nobles, Ph.D.

*"The ancestors and the womb...they're
one, they're the same.
Those in the grave, like those
who're across the sea, they're with us.
They're all the same.
The ancestors and the womb are one.
Call on your ancestors.
Let them guide you. You need their strength."*

There continues to be a cold front sweeping across Black America, moving out into the Atlantic Ocean toward the African continent.

1

STORM WATCH

Unlike most other natural phenomenon, the seasons of the year have always held a special salience in our lives. Our references to the "Winter of our discontent" or the "dead of Winter;" "the freshness and rebirth of Spring;" those "Summer breezes" of Summertime; and "those tempered days of Fall" remind us that the weather has a unique way of accessing our affective core. In fact, the relationship between the weather on any given day and our psychological disposition is highly congruent.

At a surface or common sense level, most of us recognize (when reminded) that our moods are influenced by climatic conditions. It is not uncommon for example, to feel depressed on cold, gloomy mornings or cheerful on days when the sunshine radiates with abundance. Yet, we seldom take time to analyze the universal laws which govern both nature's climatic conditions and our interaction with the environment. At times, our ambivalence toward a deeper level of

1

understanding is quite pronounced indeed. Consequently, we are rarely positioned to utilize the forces of nature to our advantage in understanding social phenomenon.

To the casual observer, a typical response to such a revelation might be "so what!" However, that casual observer must sometimes admit to being caught in a dilemma of trying to understand why some things are the way they are. Why does racism exist? Why does it seem like someone is always "mess'in" with me just because I'm different? In absence of any gems of wisdom to those queries, he or she is often forced to arrive at a conclusion which reluctantly acknowledges "it just be like that sometimes." While the willingness to acknowledge that sometimes the forces "just be" is an important survival strategy, it is equally true that one must know how to "become" in the presence of "just being." To recognize the beingness of the moment without knowing how to become in the future relegates one to a position of stagnation and potential frustration.

Knowing how "to become" is an important skill in this day and time. How do you become a man or woman in an atmosphere which seeks to strip you of your personhood? Do you accept that "it just be like that sometimes?" How do you become wise in an environment which cuts you off from any knowledge of self? Do you rationalize that "it just be like that sometimes?" How do you become more culturally congruent in a country which seeks to deny you your humanity as an African American? Should it "just be like that sometimes?"
I DON'T THINK SO!

Once you can ascertain that sometimes, "things ain't gotta be that way," you are now vulnerable to a different conceptual understanding of both your predicament, as well as your choices to be (as Spike Lee would say) "mo betta."

This conceptual shift is an important one for African Americans to adopt because life circumstances often prove individually and collectively detrimental to our people. Why, when we have access to the greatest educational institutions in this country, are we undereducated and sometimes uneducated altogether? Why, when African American purchasing power is equivalent to the ninth richest nation on earth, do our people continue to live in poverty and cling to welfare like it is our only recourse for daily sustenance? Why, when our "selves" are in need of spiritual guidance, as well as intrinsic nurturance and support, do we continue to seek extrinsic validation from material possessions? Are you feeling anxious, frustrated, depressed, or even angry? Why are you experiencing this range of feelings? Tune in to your local weather segment on the news. The answer may "just be" in the atmosphere.

The following weather forecast has been issued for African American people living in America:

Temperature: Expected highs to reach in the mid-80s, lows in the mid-to-upper 50s.

Skies: Are cloudy, compromising visibility.

Barometric Pressure: Is falling, indicating unstable weather patterns and extreme conditions.

Winds: Are blowing from the African continent at a high rate of speed.

Narrative: There continues to be a cold front

sweeping across Black America moving out into the Atlantic Ocean toward the African continent. The front is characterized by local and national policies of outright contempt and neglect; temperatures across the country are expected to drop considerably. African Americans are encouraged to be on the lookout for colliding high and low pressure weather systems, such as likely to spawn severe storms and possible hurricanes. Particular care should be taken to protect your psyche from severe storms; failure to do so could result in long-term damage to yourself and your community.

Over the past one-hundred years, scientists, researchers, meteorologists, and others have sought to investigate and understand the phenomenon of hurricane storms. In part, the investigations are fueled by curiosity as researchers seek to understand another of nature's wonders. In larger part, however, storms are studied in order to assist the world inhabitants in both predicting and adjusting to changes in climatic and weather conditions which impact their lives. Indeed, the necessity to study the phenomenon of storms was instigated by a growing recognition that the lack of preparedness could be dangerous to ones life and property. It was that fear of loss which motivated William Reid and Grady Norton to dedicate their lives to the study and forecasting of hurricane storms (Whipple, 1982).

During the same time frame, other corners of the scientific, educational, and literary communities have been wrestling with the race question as they struggle to understand the phenomenon of racism and oppression in America, as well as the

4

impact racism and oppression have had on the psyche of those who have been most oppressed, African American people. The psyche is that dynamic organization within each individual of those psychophysical systems that determine his or her unique adjustments to ones environment. In essence, it is a creative adjustment to environmental circumstances and as such, is a mode of survival. African American personality then is partly a composite of an individual's adaptation to racism in America, as well as those characteristics which are biogenetically determined by ones cultural makeup. While the recognition of the personality/environmental interaction is an important one, readers should not assume that the African American psyche can be explained so simplistically. The biogenetic/cultural makeup of the personality creates for each individual a set of needs which require fulfillment. Each individual then interacts with his/her environment in an effort to get their needs met. The cultural distinctiveness of African people colors the very nature (essence) of what the need is, as well as what is necessary to satisfy the need at a given moment. Consequently, the "personality" we experience in interacting with various African American people is the manifestation of that individual's attempt to accommodate and satisfy their needs at a basic level through their life adjustments. It is also important to understand that while individual needs may vary from person to person, there exists a set of core needs which are consistent across individuals. Included among this list are the need to sustain life (nourishment, rest, etc.), the need for growth, the need for balance and harmony, and the need for a spiritual connectedness to other living things.

Consciousness then is the quality or state of being aware of ones psychological adjustments. Therefore, ethnic consciousness is that state of being aware of oneself as an ethnic person (African American), as well as being aware of the connection between oneself and the people who share common backgrounds, characteristics, and other elements within the universe.

At the beginning of the twentieth century, it was W.E.B. DuBois who prophetically declared that the problem of this century would be the color line, the relationship of the White Western world to other people of color. His analysis suggested that race would be the most salient issue in determining the quality of relationships, distribution of power, access to opportunity, and the ability (or inability) for African American people to develop a positive sense of self in a context of color consciousness in this country. In his analysis, DuBois discussed both the racist conditions African descendants had to endure in America, as well as the process used by Black people to develop a healthy self-consciousness in the context of oppression. He writes:

"The history of the American Negro is the history of this strife - this longing to attain self-conscious manhood, to merge his double self into a better, truer self. In this merging, he wishes neither of the older selves to be lost. He would not Africanize America, for America has too much to teach the world and Africa. He would not bleach his Negro soul in the flood of White Americanism,

6

for he knows that Negro blood has a message for the world. He simply wishes to make it possible for man to be both a Negro and an American, without being cursed or spit upon by his fellows, without having the doors of opportunity closed roughly in his face."

DuBois (1903) was quick to discover that the dynamics of color consciousness would result in a cognitive and emotional battle or struggle to integrate two competing worldviews. This artificial bifurcation or "dual consciousness" as he called it, was created because of the necessity to maintain ones cultural integrity (which is African in nature) while simultaneously living in a White world which provided little or no support for that cultural authenticity.

In a similar way, Frantz Fanon (1952) recognized that the personality of the African descendent was characterized by two dimensions, one which manifests itself with other Blacks, the other which emerges as most salient when interacting with Whites. Fanon was clear in his assertion that African people behave differently with each group, and that the "self-division" was undoubtedly the result of colonial subjugation. Indeed, the sentiments of DuBois and Fanon are summarized by Ames (1950) as he so simply and eloquently declared "I've got one mind for White folks to see, another for what I know is me."

The African worldview suggests that elements within the universe are interrelated (Nobles, 1986). It is my belief in this ontological principle of "consubstantiation" which compels me to examine the similarities between the intricacies of psychological development and the complexities of atmospheric phenomenon. Much like Whites have sought to control the universe (moon, stars, life, death, planet earth, weather included), they have sought to control the political, cultural, social, and psychological socialization of African Americans. The result is a constant struggle to balance different cultural frames of reference into ones own life space. Just as storms indicate that changes in atmospheric pressure are occurring causing changes in climatic conditions, psychological storms signal that one is experiencing mild to extreme difficulties in balancing pressures between African American and European American worldviews.

There are a number of dimensions to the African worldview, which space does not permit a thorough discussion of each. For those interested in a more comprehensive discussion, they should consult Nobles (1980, 1986), Mbiti (1970), or White and Parham (1990) among others. There are, however, a number of those dimensions which bear mentioning. They include the self, survival orientation, relationship to the universe, and sense of worth. Individually and collectively, these dimensions provide a sharp contrast between the African-centered and European American-centered worldviews, while simultaneously delineating the mental struggle to balance these two perspectives into ones lifespace. In the African worldview, the self is holistic, meaning that the spiritual, cognitive (thinking), emotional, and behavioral dimension of the self are interrelated. Spirit is fundamental to everything that is, and no other dimen-

8

sion is more highly valued than another. In a European American tradition, the self is not only fragmented, but often one dimension is valued more than another (i.e. mental/rational processes over emotional/intuitive ones). The African worldview also recognized that the most salient element of existence is the collective or the group and not the individual, which is more highly valued by Europeans. Because of our belief in the interconnectedness of all things, African people relate to the universe out of a sense of harmony. European Americans, on the other hand, see themselves as the center of the universe and thus relate to the world out of a need for domination and control. Lastly, in the African-centered worldview, ones sense of worth is measured by contributions to ones family, people, and community. In the Eurocentric context, ones worth is measured by the acquisition of material goods and wealth. Pressures for African Americans to relate to the world and other people from a European perspective potentially causes severe conflict because such tendencies are contrary to ones cultural dispositions.

The concept of the hurricane storm is an appropriate allegory for two reasons. First, the components of the storm provide a precise characterization of the psychic struggle many African Americans must confront on a daily basis. Second, the devastation of the storms is analogous to what happens when the struggle for identity congruence becomes overwhelming. The hurricane storm itself is defined as a tropical cyclone with winds greater than 75 miles per hour and is typically accompanied by heavy clouds, rain, thunder, and lightning. A hurricane begins as a small tropical disturbance in the trade winds which gradually increases in strength as high pressure and low pressure combine cool high altitude winds with warm surface winds and warmer ocean temperatures to form the tropical cyclone.

Gradually, the central pressure of the cyclone begins to fall and the winds begin to flow circularly around the low pressure system. The low pressure center pulls in moist low level air and the high pressure above pulls it outward, forming a dramatic funnel shape. The eye of the storm begins to appear as characterized by little or no wind, few clouds, and warm temperatures. Once a hurricane is formed, the path the hurricane takes is influenced by the direction of the winds, usually toward higher latitudes. Ironically, while hurricanes are lethal and devastating once they come ashore, they quickly dissipate once they reach land because they lose their energy source furnished by the ocean's surface.

Symbolically, the clash of high pressure systems (African worldview) and low pressure systems (European American worldviews) represents the conflict of values and tensions between the Africentric and Eurocentric worldviews or frames of reference. The eye of the storm represents the calm we seek in trying to balance the pressures from two competing worldviews. The water mass and warm temperatures from the ocean represent both the need to seek validation from Whites, as well as the normative standards perpetuated by White society which define "appropriateness" as the degree to which one assimilates his or her values, life styles, and behaviors into what White culture suggests is legitimate. In essence, the norm becomes a White, male and female, middle to upper class standard as the reference. Clouds represent turmoil and the confusion within ones self, while land mass, whether mountainous or urban, represents changes in social norms as characterized by movement towards Africentricity, or in some cases, movement toward multiculturalism.

As one continues to explore the concept of the storm and processes of weather forecasting, we are able to see how preparing for a hurricane storm and predicting (anticipating) psychological conflict have much in common. Nowhere is this commonality more evident than in understanding storm warnings.

Experiences with oppression cause many African Americans to be hypersensitive regarding race-related issues, indeed a storm warning.

2

$$\text{————} \; : \blacklozenge : \; \text{————}$$

STORM WARNINGS

Prior to being confronted with the full force of the storm, or being compelled to search for the eye of the hurricane, each individual is likely to be presented with storm warnings. Storm warnings are defined as an alarm, summons, or signal that a storm is approaching. They serve as a caution that changes in climatic conditions (low clouds, winds, high and low pressure) are approaching and a storm is imminent. In a similar fashion, psychological storm warnings create the level of discomfort which signals that a conflict of attitudes and/or feelings which shape the "self" is occurring or about to occur. A psychological storm warning can take the form of some personal discomfort or collective social tension which is created by either positive or negative experiences in life. The personal discomfort which is experienced by an individual him/herself, or the collective social tension experienced by large groups of African Americans as a result of one individual's experi-

13

ence, can be equally significant. In the Africentric worldview, there is a collective sense of consciousness which connects us to other African people wherever they are in the diaspora. Consequently, anything experienced by one or a few members of the tribe or group is likely to be felt by other members of the collective. These experiences signal a major incongruence between what America practices and what she preaches. Sometimes, it is an intuitive sense that something is fundamentally wrong with life experiences which do not support and affirm our humanity as African Americans.

Balancing Africentric and Eurocentric worldviews is challenging to say the least. Yet each African American who lives in a world and participates in institutions controlled and/or dominated by Whites and who is relatively conscious is forced to come to grips with the reality that something is not quite right. There is internal tension and anxiety which is very real, often difficult to articulate, and sometimes unexplainable. Undoubtedly, the inevitable confrontation with a set of dualities defined by being a part of, yet apart from American society, in it but not of it, included at some level and excluded at others, is the culprit (White and Parham, 1990). This duality is at the heart of the identity struggle.

To some who live outside of the Black community, storm warnings are a curious phenomenon for the African American community to experience, since there appears to have been so much progress made since the days of slavery, Jim Crow, and the struggle for civil rights. It is undeniable that African Americans have made significant contributions to and advances in American society. In fact, a recent issue of Ebony magazine (August, 1991) spotlights some of those contributions and advances across a number of areas and disciplines. For example, the political canvas of our nation has been colored with several shades of Blackness as each candidate shares his/her vision of America with the masses. Certainly, Jesse Jackson's Presidential candidacy, Douglas Wilder's successful run at the Governor's mansion in the state of Virginia, and Thomas Bradley's longstanding tenure as Mayor of Los Angeles are among the most well known examples. African Americans are securing Congressional seats in the House of Representatives, mayoral seats in both large and small metropolitan areas, legislative seats in the state government, and even seats on the bench of the highest court in the land.

More traditional areas of success for African Americans have included entertainment (television, movies, music) and sports; indeed, our progress in these areas as well as our impact on these mediums has been and continues to be substantial. In the entertainment industry success of television programs like "The Cosby Show," "Oprah Winfrey" and "Arsenio Hall" have demonstrated how appealing Black actors and actresses can be to mainstream audiences. Film makers like Spike Lee, John Singleton, and Eddie Murphy have enjoyed similar success in the movies, reopening the doors for more Black films to be produced. Musicians such as Stevie Wonder, Patti LaBelle, Michael Jackson and Wynton Marsalis continue to impact the music industry with their creative genius, while rising stars such as rap artists Public Enemy, Ice T, Queen Latifa, Sister Soljah and Heavy D, and ballad stylists like Luther Vandross and Anita Baker continue to sparkle.

Similarly, African American athletes have dominated the fields of competition, allowing such personalities as Michael Jordan and Magic Johnson, Kirby Puckett and Cecil Fielder, Eric Dickerson and Randall Cunningham all to reportedly receive multi-million dollar contracts, while others such as Florence Griffith Joyner and Carl Lewis receive megabuck endorsements. America has also reached a point where a Black "Miss America" or "Miss USA" is no longer a once in a lifetime fluke. African American educators are becoming university and college presidents with more regularity, and even military men and women are achieving ranks of general and Chairman of the Joint Chiefs of Staff in the Armed Forces.

Truly, there has been much progress in our communities nationally, as we continue to reach milestones many thought were unattainable. But . . . at what price? While these spotlights on success are used by many in the White community and even the Black community to illustrate progress, my intuition suggests that the masses of our people will use a different yardstick to gauge whether progress for African Americans is real, or just an illusion. There is a storm warning on the horizon!

Certainly, the sacrifices of W.E.B. DuBois, Harriet Tubman, Carter G. Woodson, Marcus Garvey, Rosa Parks, Elijah Mohammed, Fannie Lou Hamer, Dr. Martin Luther King, and Malcolm

X were offered up so that we, as African American people individually, could be more than successful politicians, entertainers, and athletes. Indeed, their struggles for self-determination were intended to be the catalysts in uplifting all African Americans as a people.

Truly, these examples of success highlighted earlier stand in sharp contrast to the problems which continue to plague our community and this nation. For every successful politician, there are tens of thousands of our people who remain politically disenfranchised. For every Black million dollar athlete and entertainer, there are hundreds of thousands of our people who live in poverty. For every African American educator who has risen to become president of a college or university, or achieve some level of administrative prominence in an educational institution across this nation, there are others who point to the large percentages of Blacks who continue to be undereducated, or uneducated altogether. For every Black judge appointed or elected, he or she must view with horror the astronomical numbers of African American males and females incarcerated in our prisons and jails. And, for every successful job applicant, there are hundreds more who face no prospect of employment, or no visible means of legitimate support.

Visible signs of progress, stagnation, and even regression will continue to fuel the debate over whether African American progress is legitimate or not. Undoubtedly, it is these visible signs which are the focus of most of our attention. But I wish to focus on a different vision, one that is more latent than visible. Regardless of whether one

17

concludes that we as a people are progressing or not, each of us must play out our roles in a world where there is little or no validation for being an African American man, woman, or child. Consequently, I wonder about the psychological price we as African Americans pay to live out our lives. Whether your life is characterized by experiences with success or experiences with victimization, there is a cost for the posture we assume. Regardless of how successful we think we are, how educated we think we are, or how much money we have on deposit in our local bank, each of us knows, if only at an intuitive level, that our success is tainted by racism. Each of us believes that Rodney King, the Los Angeles Police Department's nightmare of being caught smiling on candid camera when they thought nobody was looking in March of 1991, could be any one of us. We as African Americans know all too well that no matter how prestigious the neighborhood, no matter how affluent the prep school we send our children to, the tragedy of a Korean grocer in South Central L.A. who shot and killed a young fifteen year old African American girl over a $1.79 carton of orange juice could happen to any one of our babies. Added to these tragedies is the notion that there is little justice in the world when police officers who savagely beat African American men are acquitted of police harassment charges and found not guilty, while Korean merchants who shoot and kill African American children are sentenced to probation. Ironically, African Americans who commit similar or even lesser crimes are sent directly to jail, without passing go or collecting $200.00. There are some storm warnings on the horizon!

Storm warnings are characterized by significant social events or situational phenomenon which instigate both positive and negative feelings about ourselves and other African Americans, as well as people from other cultures. For example, the lack of any substantial progress or gains by African Americans on political, educational, social, or economic issues may stimulate feelings of anger and resentment regarding unmet expectations. The Los Angeles riots in the Spring of 1992 serve as a prime example of a social movement which compels each of us to examine our thoughts, feelings, and behaviors regarding African American life in America. The physical and material violence and social unrest which characterized the riots is a reflection of the anger, despair, and hopelessness many people feel regarding their station in life. The tension stimulates personal and collective defensiveness as African Americans simultaneously recognize both the need for cultural unity among themselves, and the glaring real or perceived injustices which are perpetrated on a community by other ethnic groups.

The verdicts in the cases of Rodney King, Latasha Harlins, Bernard Getz, Yosef Hawkins, and even Mike Tyson communicate several things to African American people. First, that there is a fundamental disregard and disrespect for the lives of African American people generally, and African American males in particular. Second, there is a message that there is no real avenue to seek justice in America when law enforcement is antagonistic and brutal in their exercise of power and control. White citizens are free to practice their own brand of vigilantism on African American lives, and the judicial system is racist and blind to our needs for legitimate redress of grievances. On a more global level, these incidents underscore the fact that there are indeed two societies in America, one representing the "haves" and the other representing the "have nots." These situational phenomenon or storm warnings present themselves to African Americans, regardless of his or her social class, political party, income level, or educational attainment.

In addition to the specific incidents listed above, storm warnings are also characterized by situational phenomenon which stimulate feelings of tension and uncomfortableness. These situational phenomenon include the size and ethnic makeup of ones surroundings, response to White authority figures, racist and oppressive government leadership, social movements, and even interpersonal relationships.

Size And Ethnic Makeup
Of One's Surroundings

African Americans currently constitute approximately thirteen percent of the U.S. population. As a consequence, it is inevitable that we will find ourselves representing only a small fraction of people in particular circumstances. One cannot help but notice the underrepresentation, and that realization is usually uncomfortable. It could occur in our residential neighborhoods if they are predominately White. Or, your neighborhood may be predominately Black, but the school your youngster attends may not be. Perhaps we are lucky enough to grow up in predominately African American communities and attend predominately African American or racially mixed primary and secondary schools, but attend a college or university that is predominately White. In some instances, transitioning to a campus with five percent or less African American students out of 20,000 is traumatic when that student just completed a tenure at his school where there were more than fifty percent African American students out of 2,700. In other instances, many African Americans are successful at culturally insulating themselves until they enter the working world. There, they may find themselves being "the only one" or "one of a few" within the physical plant of that job. Or perhaps, the realization strikes you when you are on a business trip and travel on an airplane or a train where the makeup of the passengers is predominately or all White.

In some instances, feelings of alienation are enhanced when attempts by African Americans to establish what might be deemed as a "cultural comfort zone" are met with resistance. Such resistance for example could take the form of refusal to allow African Americans in predominately White settings to establish their own support groups (i.e. African American cultural clubs on a high school campus or a networking group for Black employees on the job). In other instances, such resistance could take the form of overt acts of hate and hostility as African Americans are greeted in their neighborhoods with crosses burned on their lawns, or on college campuses where racial slurs are written on walls or posted on billboards. Regardless of whether the realization that you are a minority occurs as a result of experiences in ones neighborhood, primary and secondary school, college or university, employment setting, community, or travels, the recognition is likely to stimulate feelings of uncomfortableness (anxiety), isolation, alienation, and decreased motivation to perform at ones best in that situation.

In some respects, the concept of the size and makeup of ones ethnic surroundings being anxiety provoking is hard to grasp. Yet, it does happen to many African American people, even those who frequent, work or live in areas with high concentrations of other African Americans. While a number of explanations might help to explain the sense of uncomfortableness many feel, I believe, in part, the anxiety is due to the fact that while our environments are usually desegregated, they are rarely integrated. Desegregated environments allow people to inhabit the same general space in terms of physical proximity. They don't, however, guarantee that each individual can see him or herself reflected in a meaningful way in that environment.

Response To White Authority
Interaction with authority figures is inevitable as African Americans seek to control their own life experiences. Issues of independence and autonomy versus submission to dominance are at the heart of this storm warning. Depending on ones comfort level, personal relationships, racial identity attitudes, and previous experiences with Whites, re-

sponses to White authority figures are likely to range from acquiescence to rebellion.

White authority is characterized by White people (or their agents) using power, reward, and sanctions to control the behavior of African Americans within White institutions. It is represented by city, county, and federal officials who control the politics and economics of our communities. It is represented by administrators and faculty in schools and universities who control criteria for admissions, grading, promotion, and graduation. It could be represented by supervisors on the job who control hiring, promotion, advancement and termination. It is also represented by law enforcement personnel who police our streets, judges who dispense their own brand of "justice" (just us), and even correctional officials who control our jails and other facilities for incarceration.

Unfortunately, success in negotiating ones way through interactions with White authority figures depends on how adaptable African Americans can become in meeting the expectations of those who yield power, control and influence. It was Fanon (1952) who wrote that "the colonized is elevated above his jungle status in proportion to his adoption of the mother country's cultural standards."

What makes the interactions with White authority figures problematic is the tendency for Whites and other non-Black people to view African people as "less than." The "less than" perspective which emerges from many Whites is supported by their propensity for conceptualizing anything different as being deficient or inferior. Consequently, differences in outward features like skin color, language style, etc., or more covert features like different value systems, are rarely interpreted as mere differences; more often, they place African people in a one down position.

The one down position many Whites and other non-Blacks relegate African American people to is further supported by the tendency to stereotype. Historically, Whites have cast African people in very negative ways, characterizing them for example as less intelligent, good athletes, lazy, poor communicators, militant and violent. In light of these characterizations, any behavior displayed by African American people is likely to be colored by these perceptions. Such a posture then motivates many non-Blacks to selectively attend to any shred of evidence which validates their preconceived notions about Black people.

As a result, an African American motorist who is stopped by police is viewed as potentially violent; the student who interacts with teachers, professors, or administrators is viewed as probably less intelligent, and the worker who interacts with supervisors and colleagues on the job is viewed as less capable and lazy. African people then quite naturally have a tendency to feel anxious and uncomfortable in those situations because most of us can perceive the negative ways in which many non-Black people view us.

**Racist And Oppressive
Government Leadership**

Storm warnings are also stimulated by government leadership when politicians in control implicitly and explicitly communicate a fundamental disregard for the civil and human rights of African Americans. Incidents such as a Presidential veto of the civil rights act, attempts to abolish affirmative action programs, decisions to financially support racist governments in South Africa, or proposals to cut social programs all serve as reminders that African Americans, their survival and their values are not supported within this American culture. When you have administrations in Washington or in state governments who develop no economic programs for those in need, no housing programs for those without shelter, no educational programs for those who are undereducated, and no equal opportunity programs for those who are victims of racism and discrimination in the workplace, you have a community contaminated by benign neglect.

Conflicts in values (storm warnings) are also interpreted through the actions of African American leaders themselves as the masses of people watch the lengths to which some will go to receive validation from Whites and attain some level of occupational success. Some of our leaders adopt extremely conservative postures on various political and social positions, while simultaneously denying the existence of racism and discrimination and its impact on African Americans. Such postures are assumed in order to secure seats on the Supreme Court of the United States, positions within presidential and state government cabinets, or positions of national visibility in the television and print media. Advocating positions that "African Americans are afraid of freedom and too preoccupied with racism for their own good" (Steel,

1989) go a long way towards gaining recognition and validation from Whites. What is important to remember however, is that regardless of whether you agree or disagree with a particular position on a certain issue, the fact that a leader's posture communicates a disregard for or lack of support for African American life and ideals creates a dissonance in the minds of many Black people.

Social Movements
Sometimes storm warnings are characterized by social movements which stimulate feelings ranging from pride to feelings of anger and degradation. These social movements often serve as a reminder about the inequities in American society. From a positive Black perspective, a social movement might include the Presidential candidacy of an African American politician who urges Black people to change their condition in life through voter registration and the ballot. Social movements are also characterized by community activism as Black leaders including Reverend Jesse Jackson, Minister Louis Farrakhan, José Williams, Dr. Benjamin Hooks, Reverend Al Sharpton, Mike McGee, Maxine Waters, Coretta Scott King, and Sonja Sanchez encourage African Americans to move towards self-determination.

Whether it is the new spirit of Africentricity which is sweeping this nation in the 90s, the civil rights and Black power movements of the 50s and 60s, or the Garvey movements of the 1920s and 30s, African American people are constantly being challenged to think differently about life in America in what seems to be thirty year cycles. Occasion-

26

ally, even military conflicts represent social movements which serve as storm warnings. Whether the Civil War, World Wars I or II, the Korean Conflict, Vietnam, or Operation Desert Storm in the Persian Gulf, the race equity question is never far from Black people's thinking. Questions about whether to fight and die for a country which oppresses you, feelings of anger and resentment at the second class status Blacks are assigned, the refusal to accept segregated or unequal accommodations, or take orders from someone you perceive as a racist, highlight the cognitive, affective, and behavioral dimensions of the psychological dissonance.

Negative social movements are equally stirring as African Americans are forced to confront overt racist White supremacist groups like the Ku Klux Klan, White Knights, or the Aryan Nation. It could be the political candidacy of a David Duke in Louisiana, the ultra-conservative views of a Jesse Helms in Carolina, the states of Arizona and New Hampshire refusal to acknowledge the birthday of Dr. Martin Luther King, or the lack of significant numbers of Whites rising up to condemn real or perceived racist practices in their own communities. African Americans read hate on the faces at Howard Beach, Bensenhurst, Forsyth County, Georgia and even Simi Valley, California. The hostility communicated by people in those communities and projected on to African Americans and other people of color create unnecessary hypersensitivity. Clearly, there are some storm warnings on the horizon.

Interpersonal Relations

Situational phenomenon which serve as storm warnings also include relationships with others. Sometimes the dissonance we feel in balancing different cultural worldviews is stimulated through the interaction we experience in developing inter-personal and intrapersonal relations with other cultural groups. The relationships we ultimately develop are in part a result of decisions we make and preferences we express toward people them-selves and physical characteristics they repre-sent. Decisions on who to establish a friendship with, who to socialize with, who to romance, who to consult and network with, and who to affiliate with are all impacted by ones cultural worldview.

Some of the factors we debate which ultimately serve as manifestations of our identity resolution include: same race versus other race partners, preferences for race with light, brown, or dark skin tones, and African versus European facial features; highly educated versus uneducated people; and preferences for persons from different social and occupational classes. For example, in-ternal conflicts and tension arise when African Americans decide to pursue an intimate relation-ship with a non-African American (the Jungle Fever phenomenon), to affiliate with a profes-sional organization which is all or predominately White, or to allow ones children to date interracially. Dissonance is sometimes created around the simplest of interactions like should I be seen having lunch with a friend who is non-Black. In some respects, the stress points in inter-personal relations are not necessarily conscious decisions. Rather, tension emerges as the result of an intuitive recognition of some anxiety or uncomfortableness associated with the decision. Indeed, there are some storm warnings on the horizon.

In some respects, characterizing dissonance in interpersonal relationships in the context of only African American and Caucasian relations is limiting. Indeed, anxiety is also felt as African Americans interact with other ethnic groups as well. In fact, I have found that tensions for African Americans permeate relations with Asians (i.e. Japanese, Korean) and Chicano/Latinos (i.e. Mexican Americans) among others. This observation is not meant to imply that relationships with African Americans as a whole and other ethnic groups are poor, or that African Americans harbor any particular ill feelings towards them. On the contrary, there are a number of circumstances which point to very positive relations between these groups.

There are, however, a number of specific and general incidents which are less than positive. For example, recent history has documented several racially derogatory statements being made by high ranking officials of the Japanese government about African Americans in the United States. How does the interpretation of these statements by African Americans influence their relationships with other Japanese Americans with whom they interact on a daily basis? I would speculate that some African Americans wonder whether their Japanese American acquaintances or other Japanese Americans in general share such views. In another example, tensions between African Americans and members of the Korean communities across this nation have also risen in recent years. At one level, the tension seems to be reflective of a fundamental distrust and outright fear of each other. Incidents such as the Korean grocer in South Central Los Angeles who shot and killed a 15 year old African American girl over a $1.79 carton of orange juice, or African American youth and adults who targeted Korean businesses in the Black community during the April 1992 uprising in Los Angeles, speak directly to the hostility and anger which color the interactions between these two groups. How does the knowledge of these events influence the affective responses of Blacks who interact with many Koreans on a daily basis? I suspect that it creates a level of discomfort in many settings where the two groups interact.

The dynamics of oppression have also impacted relations between African Americans and Latinos. The scarcity of resources in the inner cities and rural communities of this nation have forced these two groups to more actively compete for a smaller share of available opportunities in employment, education, politics, and other services. The competition often creates feelings of anxiety and tension, which in some respects is due to the feeling that each should somehow be given a kind of "favored minority status" by the mainstream White society. Such status, however, while symbolically important, often relegates each group to a position of questioning their inherent worth and esteem when compared to the other. Such comparisons help to stimulate the feelings of discomfort and tension which serve as a reminder that there are some storm warnings on the horizon.

Summary

The nature of experiences with oppression cause many African Americans to be hypersensitive regarding race-related issues. Indeed, storm warnings serve as a signal or alarm that either personal anxiety or collective social tension is being felt by the person as the result of some experiences or situational phenomenon. Despite the mild to moderate discomfort, the warning is necessary because it serves as a preview to the pending storm.

One measure of a full force storm is African Americans believing that their worth and sense of self should be measured with a Eurocentric yardstick.

3

THE FULL FORCE
OF THE STORM

Hurricanes are among nature's most destructive forces. Once fully formed, they can reach speeds in excess of 120 miles per hour, creating extremely high winds, rough seas, tidal waves, and torrential rains. If hurricanes strike land, the force can be devastating and lethal in terms of property damage and loss of life.

Psychological storms can be mentally devastating, wreaking havoc on our total selves. Balancing the pressures (high) between Africentric cultural values and dispositions with those pressures (low), created by living in a society dominated by Whites and Eurocentric values is quite a challenge. The sense of incongruence is further enhanced if African Americans believe that their worth and sense of self should be measured against a Eurocentric normative standard (ocean, water mass). Granted, ones identity and sense of self is influenced both by personal opinions of self, as well as validation and feedback from significant others. However, if

African American sources of validation emanate from the White community rather than the African American community, the degree of incongruence between ones real self and the self one tries to become is more pronounced.

Clearly, the inclusion-exclusion dilemma is at the heart of the struggle for congruence. White and Parham (1990) speak to this issue clearly as they write that each African American must achieve some balance between African American and European American values within their own psychological consciousness. If one attempts to avoid contact with, or deny either worldview, he or she risks the restriction of choices and options on either side, stunting of personal growth, limitations of interpersonal relations, and restrain of economic opportunities. If African Americans adopt a lifestyle which emphasizes Eurocentric values of individualism, competition, emotional isolation, power, control and dominance, he or she may achieve success at a cost of being alienated from friends, peers, and elders in the African American community.

Historically, these friends, peers, and elders value genuineness, cooperation, and emotional interrelatedness. These individuals may also be relegated to a life of confusion and alienation because their attitudes and behaviors are inconsistent with their cultural essence. Ironically, that cultural isolation one may feel is likely to be a double-edged sword in that he or she is not likely to receive full or genuine acceptance and validation from the White world either. On the other hand, if an African American man or woman completely ignores the values or lessons which facilitate progress in the occupational mainstream, he or she will have dramatically reduced the available range of options and choices and the material quality of life associated with those options (White and Parham, 1990).

The full force of the hurricane storm is the symbolic representation of the tension and confusion African Americans feel when recognizing that whether we embrace our culture totally and restrict options and choices in the White world, or deny our cultural makeup in favor of the prospect of material success and White validation, there is no way to escape feeling oppressed. In an attempt to avoid the extremes of either cultural value system, some African Americans decide to take refuge in the middle ground between each worldview. In essence, it is analogous to what DuBois (1903) described as the "twoness" one feels as two warring idols (one African, one American) struggle for control. This phenomenon of the dual consciousness can be very stressful and mentally devastating if the person is unclear about where to find psychological peace and comfort.

The Path Of Destruction

In the African worldview, the "self" is viewed as holistic. That means, it is impossible to impact one dimension of the self and not impact the total organism. Consequently, psychological storms impact the cognitive (thoughts), affective (feelings), and response (behaviors) dimensions of the self such that the person impacted thinks, feels, and responds to issues simultaneously. Cognitively, storms create confusion, self-doubt, insecurity, and dissonance (conflict), especially if the identity resolution strategy is skewed toward a Eurocentric perspective. To the degree that African Americans embrace a more Africentric worldview, then the cognitive dimensions of the storm are likely to simulate thoughts of acceptance, determination, and mental resistance.

Affectively, storms can instigate feelings of stress, anxiety (mild discomfort), resentment, anger, guilt, mistrust, self-rejection, shame, embarrassment, sadness, hurt, hostility, and depression (burnout). It is equally likely that feelings of self-pride, joy, general comfort, resilience, love, laughter, satisfaction, excitement and revitalization can occur if the storm centers itself in an Africentric hemisphere (worldview). Behaviorally, psychological storms can influence a person to respond to their life conditions by isolating and alienating them. That isolation could occur in the White community as a person seeks refuge from the storm, or the isolation could be characterized by confining and restricting oneself to Black oriented activities and clubs within the Black community.

The direction that a hurricane travels in some respects is unpredictable. Similarly, predicting the path of a psychological storm can be equally perplexing. There is some psychological literature, however, which seems to capture the essence of the storm and hypothesize about its direction. Tropical storms have been a part of nature since time began. Likewise, psychological storms are not a recent phenomenon either. In fact, the historical legacy of African people in America has been characterized by an overt friction or tension. On one side, that tension was created by European American attempts to enslave African people and also strip African men, women, and children of their cultural heritage and force them to assimilate to a White cultural standard. On the other side, the stress point became the mental and behavioral resistance by African people as they sought to maintain their cultural identification and cultural heritage. The psychological tug-of-war between African people and Europeans has resulted in an identity development process characterized by varying degrees of Black people's identification with and resistance to adopting White cultural values.

Recognizing that attempts to strip African Americans of their ethnic identity is as fundamental to life in America as anything else, several authors have articulated stage theories which describe the process of deculturalization and then cultural revitalization (Cross, 1971, 1978; Thomas, 1971; Williams, 1981). These theories are collectively known as models of psychological Nigrescence. They describe a process by which African Americans react to oppressive conditions in America by moving through various identity states characterized by a continuum of pro-White/anti-Black feelings through feelings of self-pride and pro-Blackness.

Cross (1971, 1978), for example, hypothesized about the identity resolution process by suggesting that African Americans move through four distinct psychological stages: **Pre-encounter, Encounter, Immersion-Emersion,** and **Inter-**

nalization as they struggle for self-actualization under conditions of oppression. In the **Pre-Encounter stage,** an individual is prone to view the world from a White frame of reference as he or she thinks, acts, and behaves in ways that devalue or deny their Blackness. During the **Encounter stage,** an individual experiences a startling personal or social event which challenges their belief in a pre-encounter orientation (they discover that racism does in fact exist). In the **Immersion-Emersion stage,** the individual begins to immerse him or herself into their own African culture believing that everything of relevance in life must be related to their Blackness. This stage is also characterized by a tendency to denigrate White people while simultaneously glorifying African American people. In the **Internalization stage,** a person has developed an inner security and self-confidence with their African American culture.

In analyzing the stages, one can begin to see the distinctiveness between the identity states. Initially, there is a strong "identification with the oppressor" phenomenon where a Black person's sense of self is totally related to the acquisition of validation and approval from Whites. This stage is analogous to the cultural sell out or "Uncle Tom" stereotype in our community. Gradually, the individual begins to recognize through experience that the only person forgetting that he or she is African American is himself. The interesting thing about these encounters or social phenomenon is the lack of reliability in predicting which encounter or how many experiences with racism will be most salient to a person's identity resolution struggle. For some

African Americans, one incident may be sufficient; for others, several incidents may be required to provide that necessary challenge to a belief in a European American worldview.

The vulnerability to change ones worldview will be influenced by the degree of psychological defensiveness present at the time of each encounter. If the degree of defensiveness is low, then the prospect of change is heightened by one or a few incidents. If the degree of defensiveness is more pronounced, then several encounters may be necessary to challenge a person's Eurocentric belief system. Once a person begins to reinterpret the world from a Black frame of reference, their degree of cultural identification will be intense. In time however, the intensity may decrease or remain the same as each person becomes more secure in their identity and more grounded in the principles which provide the foundation for understanding their true self.

While most of the Nigrescence literature describes the progression from attitudes of self-denigration to self-pride in a linear fashion, it is also possible that the psychological storms one experiences may leave a person stagnated in one of the stages described above or may stimulate a recycling through the stages a second time after an initial cycle has already been completed (Parham, 1989). The recycling phenomenon is a particularly interesting one because it may provide the most accurate portrayal of identity resolution over time. The fact that a person will experience several weather storms in any one season of the year seems rather obvious. Likewise, the possibility

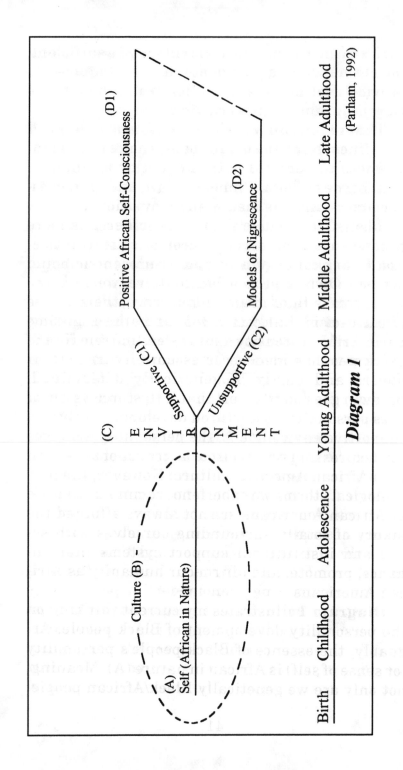

(C)

E
N
V
I
R
O
N
M
E
N
T

Supportive (C1)

Unsupportive (C2)

(D1)

Positive African Self-Consciousness

(D2)

Models of Nigrescence

Culture (B)

(A)
Self (African in Nature)

Birth   Childhood   Adolescence   Young Adulthood   Middle Adulthood   Late Adulthood

(Parham, 1992)

Diagram 1

that a person may experience several psychological storms during any one stage of the developmental life cycle is equally possible. The notion of recycling then suggests that African Americans may move through the Nigrescence stages more than once during their life, and that each initiation into the process is influenced by an interaction between social phenomenon and personal/developmental life issues and transitions.

While Cross' stage theory and other models of Nigrescence describe a process of self-actualization under conditions of oppression, they should not be interpreted to mean that everyone's identity, or ones total identity is merely a reaction to White racism. Baldwin (1985) and others (Akbar, 1979; Azibo, 1989) have suggested that the core of Black people's identity is essentially African in nature and partly biogenetically determined. Baldwin goes on to assert that if the core system of ones personality is nurtured developmentally in a supportive environment, the personality achieves full expression in terms of a congruent pattern with African American culture. However, the psychological storms we experience remind us that we as African Americans are not always afforded the luxury of totally surrounding ourselves with social and institutional support systems that enhance, promote, and affirm our humanity as African Americans.

Diagram 1 illustrates my current thinking on the personality development of Black people. Arguably, the essence of Black people's personality (or sense of self) is African in nature (A). Meaning, not only are we genetically Black/African people,

but our personalities are "spiritness" made evident (Myers, 1988). That spiritness (spirituality)
or life force is fundamental to everything that is in
the universe. It reveals itself both through our
consciousness (including our conception of God
the Creator) as well as through our recognition
that each of us owes our very existence to the
African collective (parents and elders, ancestors,
and those not yet born). Our spiritual essence is
surrounded by a veil of culture (B) which as Nobles
(1984) explains, provides a general design for living and a pattern for interpreting ones reality.
These cultural rules for living are intended to
facilitate the full expression of ones spiritual essence (or sense of self).

Recognizing that the self we develop (not necessarily who we are) is influenced by the environmental context (C) to which it is exposed, we then
begin to gain some insight into how various models
of personality development account for differen-
tial manifestations of who one becomes. For example, if as Baldwin (1985) asserts, the person
grows up and is nurtured in an environment which
is supportive (C1), then the likely outcome will be
a personality which could be described as a positive African self-consciousness (D1). Such might
be characterized by a strong identification with
African cultural values, a recognition of ones connectedness to the Creator, feelings of self (individual and collective) love and self-pride, and an
exercise of behavior which supports, affirms, and
promotes the survival, enhancement, and eleva-
tion of ones self and ones people. If however the
environment is unsupportive, denigrating, oppres-

sive and even hostile (C2) and affirmation and validation for ones existence is lacking or non-existent, then a negative sense of self is a likely outcome with the models of Nigrescence (D2) (i.e. Cross) serving as an appropriate explanation of the resolution process that self will likely experience.

The Hurricane Storm is a symbolic representation of the psychic struggle African Americans endure.

4

---- : ◆ : ----

THE EYE OF THE HURRICANE: MANAGING ANXIETY

The inevitable discomfort when juggling two worldviews will make African Americans desire to search for the eye of the hurricane compelling. In the wake of the force of the psychological storms which can be severe, individuals often seek to find a place of momentary calm. For many African Americans, that place is represented by the eye of the storm. The eye of the hurricane is an area characterized by a hole in the center of this tropical cyclone where light winds, calm, very few clouds, and no precipitation are its trademark. Psychologically, attempts to create a safe haven from whatever anxiety one may feel in balancing different worldview perspectives (high and low pressure systems) result in individuals making less than creative adjustments.

Clinically, anxiety is defined as an abnormal and overwhelming sense of apprehension and fear. Because anxiety often generates a high degree of discomfort, most people, and African Americans are no exception, unconsciously develop strategies for managing these uncomfortable feelings. These less than creative adjustments often take the form of some interesting decision points and personality profiles. These outcome decisions and personality personas characterize African American life in the eye of the storm. I hesitate to classify these persona we adopt as typologies or rigid categories. Rather, they should be viewed as fluid and flexible attitudes with permeable boundaries which allow for movement within (increases or decreases in intensity) or between (one category to the next) states.

Some of the less than creative behavioral and attitudinal adjustments I have observed as African Americans seek to manage their discomfort in balancing two worldviews are as follows:

Pass'in - Attempts to understate, down-play, or otherwise camouflage ones African American makeup. These individuals try to embrace and adopt the characteristics of the dominant culture. Every fiber of their being suggests that they want to be White, from their wardrobe, hairstyle, language style, peer group, spouse/partner, and professional affiliations and political views. They have incorporated and clearly project negative attitudes and feelings towards self and other African Americans.

Cultural Confusion - A state of disorder and failure to differentiate oneself as an African American. The individual does not identify with any cultural worldview or value system and is prone to want to be identified as just another "human being." If active at all in any community, they will avoid culturally specific causes in favor of more race neutral movements like animal rights or environmental concerns.

On Being Fashionably Black - This individual profile characterizes those African Americans who try their best to "straddle the fence" between competing worldviews. They want to be "Black enough" to feel a sense of cultural integrity, but not so Black as to warrant unwanted attention or offend White people from whom they seek approval and validation. They identify with and sometimes worship the personalities of historical and contemporary Black leaders, but have difficulty operationalizing the principles of the leader's message into their own life space. For example, they might wear a Malcolm X hat or a button but will not struggle for freedom "by any means necessary."

Blacker Than Thou Thinking - This thought process emerges out of a deep-seated identification with anything and everything that is African. "Blacker than thou" thinking is an attempt to help an African American man or woman feel comfortable with their own ethnic consciousness by confronting other African Americans about their perceived lack of identity. There is an inability to accept and/or tolerate other African Americans if their views, behaviors, and language style do not meet rigid standards for ones personal definition for Blackness.

The Curse of Material Possession and Success - Because of the historical connection between poverty and Black people, and power, material possession and White people, many African

Americans are uncomfortable surrounding themselves with "the trappings of success." Dissonance and conflict are created as many ponder questions like: whether or not to buy an expensive automobile; whether or not to live in a particular neighborhood; whether or not to wear expensive jewelry; or whether or not to frequent a particular establishment. Individuals who struggle with this affliction somehow believe that their ethnic consciousness is totally connected with the car they drive, the clothes they wear, and the money they spend.

This perspective acknowledges that the "curse" is a particular consequence of having access to the resources necessary to buy material goods. It is also important to recognize, however, that the obsession with material possessions also negatively impacts those who have limited or no access to resources to purchase expensive items. Many African Americans have a sense of self which is compromised by a belief that they are not as good as others who have some wealth.

Color and Feature Consciousness in our Relationships - Relationships and the mates we select are a natural extension of ourselves. Too often, our anxieties in balancing different worldviews are played out in our opinions and choices of mates. Sometimes our desires to embrace Eurocentric values and people result in the selection of Whites as relationship partners. In some respects, those selections provide some African Americans with a false sense of security because their choices are rooted in rationalizations which are questionable. Many Black men rationalize their selections of White women on the basis of three positions. They include "she accepts me for who I really am," "she is more sexually open to exploration," and "she is a way for me to possess something of the White man's." For many Black women, they rationalize their selections of White men on the basis of "he can better provide (economically) for me" or "he knows how to treat me like a woman." In other cases, some Black men and women claim to ignore color, choosing instead to appreciate the other personal qualities of the person to which they are attracted. Despite these common rationalizations, Black men and women who select Whites as relationship partners may unconsciously be accepting personal love and affection from individual Whites as evidence of their worthiness to receive approval and validation from the general White European American culture. It is also important to note that there may be some African Americans who choose relationship partners without focusing on his or her race. Choices may be more a matter of mutual attraction unrelated to skin color, rather than a personal reflection of one's identity. Sometimes we choose African American mates but scrutinize potential according to that person's degree of likeness to European features (light skin tones, texture of hair, etc.). In other instances, mates are deliberately selected because they embody very African features; consequently, a person's view of her or himself is enhanced by identifying with a mate who is more Black in appearance.

In examining the thoughts, feelings and behaviors which characterize ones personality makeup, self-rejection can often lead to questions regarding why we as African Americans develop the type of coping strategies listed above. I believe that it is important to remember that the thinking, feeling, and response dimensions of our personalities are in tune with our core needs at a basic level. Consequently, all behaviors (including thoughts and feelings) are functional; meaning they serve a deeper purpose which may be more psychologically latent than visible. It is important, however, to recognize that the strategies listed above are attempts by African Americans to cope with the tension and anxiety we often feel in balancing different worldviews. Given these set of circumstances, the question which remains is how can African Americans begin to make more creative adjustments in balancing the anxiety they experience in everyday life? It is also important to remember that while the eye of the hurricane represents a temporary calm, one soon realizes that the calm is only an illusion. Gradually, the illusion of calm begins to evaporate as winds begin to increase, and the storm's movement continues to wreak havoc and destruction on anything in its path. In point of fact, the eye of the hurricane serves as sort of a warning that the storm (psychological dissonance) is still very much present. Ultimately, each individual must understand that the safest place to be is not in the eye of the storm, but out of the storm altogether.

Cloudy Vision
The cloudiness which surrounds the psychic storms we experience creates an enormous amount

49

of visual obstruction. The obstruction prevents each of us from recognizing the cause of the storm, the amount of psychic devastation we have been subjected to, and the continual consequences to the psyche if the storm persists. The absence of clouds in the eye of the storm creates a delusional belief system which allows one to assume that the less than creative adjustments one adopts are in fact adequate coping measures. Nothing could be further from the truth. Since many of the personality types described previously rely on a European American frame of reference or worldview, an African American can never find real or genuine self-fulfillment using that normative standard.

The negative consequences of psychological and cultural confusion is similar to the devastation left by a hurricane.

5

SURVEYING THE DEVASTATION

In the aftermath of any hurricane, one can easily see the amount of destruction and devastation caused by the storm. In some cases, communities and their residents emerge relatively unaffected by the hazardous weather conditions. More often than not, however, the toll is characterized by damage to residential and commercial structures, trees and landscape, personal possessions (i.e. automobiles), and even loss of life. As each of us emerges from our places of refuge, we stand in awe or cultural shock at the awesome power of nature's phenomenon. In a similar way, we must begin to examine and measure the consequences of psychological storms, where attempts to balance competing worldviews exacts a price which is equally high.

Accurately reading weather equipment used to predict storms (i.e. radar) and appropriately surveying the devastation requires an effective interpretive lens through which to view both atmospheric phenomenon and the consequences of a major storm. That interpretive lens should be an Africentric (African centered) perspective. Developing an Africentric perspective requires first and foremost that a person be knowledgeable about African values, traditions, history and culture, and that he or she embrace that knowledge as the foundation of their worldview. Once endorsed, those cultural norms must then become the lens through which his or her perceptions of reality are shaped and colored.

Several authors have identified values and assumptions which characterize the behaviors and styles of African Americans (Nobles, 1980; White, Parham, and Parham, 1980; White and Parham, 1990). These styles of responding to our reality in America can be contrasted across several dimensions, allowing for an analysis of our behavior against a backdrop of worldview belief systems. This behavioral analysis is important because as Myers (1988) asserts, human behavior is spiritness made evident. Thus, through analyzing behaviors people provide us with insight into what is in their consciousness. Indeed, "Ideas are the substance of behavior" (Nobles, 1986).

The following chart allows for a comparison of Eurocentric and Africentric values which permeate the cognitive, affective, and behavioral dimensions of our personality. It is my belief that the degree of psychological and even behavioral devastation one experiences will correspond to the degree of inclusion of Eurocentric values into ones life. If your sense of self is devoid of spirituality (spiritness), if your contribution is only to "self" and not others, if you only compete and never cooperate, if your approach to life is based on control of things and people rather than living in harmony, and if your sense of worth is externally derived and based on material wealth rather than on self-knowledge and community uplifting, then your personal incongruence will be substantial.

Eurocentric	Dimensions	Africentric
Dualistic/Fragmented	Self	Holistic/Spiritness Thoughts, Emotions, Behaviors are Interrelated
Suppressed in Favor of Rational Imperatives	Feelings	Expressed/Legitimate Creativity and Intuitiveness
Individual/Competitive Autonomous	Survival	Collective - "I am-We are" Support, Interdependence, Unity, Cooperative Economics
Written/Formal/ Detached	Language	Oral/Informal/Interconnectedness Between Speaker and Listener
Metric Units/A Commodity to be Invested, Oriented to the Future	Time	Events/Experience/ Orientation from Past to Present
Control-Forces of Nature/Other Human Beings	Universe	Harmony-with Nature/Other Human Beings, Need for Balance, Self-determination
Final	Death	Extension of Life
Material Possessions/ Externally Derived/ Individual Achievement	Worth	Contributing to the Up-lifting of ones People, Internal Knowingness, Collective Work and Responsibility

In essence, I am suggesting that the latent devastation created by psychological conflicts is sometimes represented by the tendency to define ones self and validate ones existence against the Eurocentric normative standard. Myers' (1988) supports this contention as she writes:

". . . values and attitudes perpetuated by White society have had a detrimental impact on the Black community. The primary Eurocentrically oriented values of materialism, individualism, and competition foster orientations which are in opposition to the ones necessary to liberate the lives and minds of oppressed people."

There are many African Americans in our communities who can successfully weather the storms and remain relatively unscathed because of their anchoring in an Africentric value system. There are too many others, however, who experience the negative consequences of psychological and cultural confusion of their adoption and/or socialization to a European value system. Unfortunately, adopting non-African values will not allow one to better cope with the ravages of oppression and discrimination. And, as Akbar (1981) has pointed out "Oppression is an unnatural human phenomenon which stimulates unnatural human behavior." Some of these consequences include family conflict and parental neglect, Black on Black crime, the negative name game, and compromised male/female relationships.

For example, to the degree that parents and other adults experience significant difficulty in coping with the psychological trauma of life in

America, it is likely that their children and other adults will be affected as well. Parents and significant others who cannot successfully combat (confront) Eurocentric impositions in their lives will have a difficult time teaching their children how to cope with racism and oppression. My observations as a clinician have revealed several maladaptive tendencies which by way of example invite family conflict and improper child socialization.

Quite naturally, an inability to be respected and validated for who one is stimulates feelings of anger. Because expressing anger directly to White authority figures can bring unwanted consequences, that anger is often misdirected at family members or at our children. Too many African American children are cursed at, physically abused, mentally abused, and grow up in an environment void of the emotional richness and vitality required to develop and sustain a healthy sense of self. In addition, substantial increases in violence within families perpetrated by other family members may be a direct consequence of the misdirected anger, rage, frustration, and hostility African Americans feel when confronted with oppressive situations.

Another maladaptive tendency is the propensity for substance use and abuse. In many cases, use of alcohol and narcotics becomes a self-medicating prescription to dull the pain and frustration one feels. To the degree that a caregiver is regularly intoxicated, they're not only mentally absent from and out of touch with a child's needs, but they also are not providing the type of role model a child needs to experience. Once a child consistently sees their parent(s) using alcohol, drugs, etc. to cope with life's pressures, it increases the likelihood that he or she (the child) will begin to look outside of their own selves for comfort and relief rather than within themselves in search of their own spiritual essence.

Another consequence of the psychological and cultural confusion is Black on Black violence and crime. To some, the escalation of this phenomenon in our community represents attempts to survive in an otherwise hostile environment. In my opinion, however, the tendency to victimize your own people is a reflection of both deep-seated hatred and disdain we unconsciously feel for ourselves, and a commentary on our inability to recognize how the dynamics of oppression and modern day slavery create divisiveness within our own community and pits us against each other for material rewards. That internalized negative self-image is a direct consequence of an over-identification with a Eurocentric value system and worldview. These values include controlling people and resources at all costs, individual centeredness, intense competition, and developing a sense of worth which is externally derived through the acquisition of material wealth.

In some respects, violence in our community is represented by the warring between gangs. Any daytime or nightly newscast will highlight this distressing phenomenon. We watch our children engage in behaviors which have them killing each other over "turf" and colors, selling drugs to each other to support their vision of "living large," extorting money from each other for protection, and committing homicide against each other to prove one's loyalty to a gang or for reasons of retribution and retaliation. Unfortunately, the violence in our community is not limited to our youth. Data clearly shows that crimes against African Americans by African Americans are committed across all age levels and geographic neighborhoods.

We should also remind ourselves that "violence" is not limited to the physical realm. Since violence is defined as "an intensely destructive action or force," anything which proves destructive to our community can be so classified. Child neglect, disrespect for elders, antagonistic relations between males and females and children growing up without fathers in the home or otherwise involved in their lives are incidents which prove destructive to the Black family.

Teachers who provide no intellectual stimulation for our children, students who care more about sports and games than scholastic excellence and knowledge, and degreed professionals who contribute their expertise to White institutions and nothing to their own are all guilty of robbing our community of its intellectual resources.

Community residents who spend their money everywhere but in their own neighborhoods, Black business owners who give nothing back to the communities who support them, and the more economically advantaged in our community who desperately try to distance themselves from those who are less fortunate are all examples of economic violence in our communities.

Politicians whose rhetoric for media sake far

outdistance any service to their communities, other elected officials who compromise their pledges of reform in order to gain re-election from a non-African American constituency, and Black electorates who sit home rather than cast any vote and voice their power of preference are all examples of political violence in our communities.

The psychic devastation is also represented by a resolution of internal conflicts which stimulates cognitive movement towards a polarity which reflects self-hatred rather than self-love. Parham (1990) in a text he coauthored with Dr. Joseph White entitled *The Psychology of Blacks: An African-American Perspective* provides a conceptual framework of this dilemma by suggesting that as long as African Americans are confronted with racist and oppressive conditions in their lives, and are confronted with questions of how much to compromise their cultural integrity in favor of assimilation, they will struggle with issues (themes) of identity and self-worth, physical makeup, and ego ideal. The contrasting polarities include: **self-differentiation versus preoccupation with assimilation;** where an individual struggles with a sense of worth and validation which emerges from the African worldview rather a constant search for White validation. **Body transcendence versus pre-occupation with body image;** where one seeks to become comfortable and accepting of ones African physical features instead of compulsively trying to lighten skin tones, straighten hair textures, and re-contour facial features to approximate a European standard of attractiveness. **Ego transcendence versus self-**

absorption; where personal ego strength is developed through contributing to ones people and ones community rather than a personal obsession with personal gratification and self-aggrandizement.

The psychic devastation can also be seen through the ways African Americans greet each other, refer to each other, and generally converse with each other. The assumption here is that the practice of communicating is a dramatic presentation of ones personhood to those who share a background of similar acculturation (Holt 1975). Generally, African American people converse with each other in ways which communicate interest, respect, and caring. There are, however, too many of us who verbally and non-verbally communicate a fundamental disregard and disrespect for African American people and ourselves. Disregard for others is communicated through our references we make in describing African Americans as "niggers" and "mother f_ _ _ _ r." In some cases, the references are deliberate characterizations of other African people. In other instances, the negative references are so ingrained and natural to us that we are not even aware of how often we use them. Clearly, images of ourselves are in need of repair when we constantly characterize our women as "bitches" and our men as "dogs," especially when the references are preceded by the adjective "Black." And sadly, the tendency to label ourselves in a negative way is just as pronounced. One has only to consult a few of our recording artists who designate themselves as "Niggers With Attitudes (NWA)" and "Bitches With Problems (BWP)" to recognize this truth.

The psychic devastation can also be analyzed via the difficulties many African American males and females are having in developing healthy productive relationships. White and Parham (1990) have suggested that ideal relationships between African American males and females are characterized by the values of interdependence, cooperation, mutual respect, and an absence of rigid sex role distinctions regarding economics, household responsibilities, and social roles (page 139). Indeed, relationships that are built on a bond of sharing, nurturance, tenderness, and appreciation have a strong psychological foundation necessary to cope with the social and economic stresses that usually confront Black males and females. In contrast, there are too many African American male-female relationships that are characterized by self-centeredness, faulty expectations, exploitation, deception, and a lack of trust. Indeed, these characteristics are preventing males and females from achieving relationship satisfaction.

The devastation in our communities can also be seen through the lack of support African American people provide each other in the world of work. Many African Americans in hiring positions often find it difficult to endorse or advocate for other African American job candidates. Sometimes the lack of support is stimulated by personal anxieties related to a belief that "another Black person" might jeopardize ones position within a company. In other instances, the anxiety is instigated by a fear of antagonizing White supervisors, colleagues, and even subordinates who might question why one would support another African American candidate.

Unfortunately, the psychic devastation which compels too many African Americans to distance themselves from African American oriented business supports (attorneys, physicians, accountants, managers, etc.) is not restricted to the wealthiest among us. The belief that White people, White products, and White businesses are somehow better than those in the African American community permeates every level of the economic strata. Too many of us sell our houses without considering using a Black real estate agent. Too many of us deposit our monies in banks with no Black ownership or no commitment to providing loans and other banking services to the African American community. Too many of us purchase automobiles, clothing, and other retail merchandise without the thought of giving those dollars salespeople earn through commissions, to an African American. Too many of us hire contractors for work around our houses and avoid soliciting bids from African Americans who can provide the same service.

Curiously, even the supposedly "most successful" among us seem to believe that their continued success is tied to surrounding themselves with primarily White people. I often view with irony how, for example, television personalities, entertainers, and athletes promote, finance, and lend their names to sporadic functions designed to help the Black community. On the surface, that individual seems to care deeply about and support his/her community. However, a closer look reveals that their support may be tangential. I believe that "your heart" is not restricted to what one finances, but who one trusts to negotiate their contracts, handle their business affairs (i.e., agents), and spend their money. For too many of our African American entertainment personalities, those duties involving business and legal affairs are relegated to White people. This observation is not meant to suggest that any group is incapable of handling these responsibilities; it is meant to state emphatically that there are African American professionals who can, but are never given the opportunity.

Indeed, surveying the devastation created by these psychological storms we experience can be eye opening. As one views with awe the depth of destruction, it is not uncommon to wonder in retrospect if there was anything that could have been done to protect our psyche from the ravages of the storm? Listen to the weathermen, those elders, healers, psychologists, and others who understand the climatic conditions we currently live under.

Knowledge of ones culture and history is paramount to the fortification of our psyche and a necessary tool for weathering life's storms.

6

PREPARING FOR THE NEXT
STORM: FORTIFICATION

Scientists and meteorologists have become much better at understanding and predicting storm phenomenon. Consequently, they are much more adept at both warning those who might be affected by the storms, and protecting those who experience the storm from severe harm. Unfortunately, many of us in the African American community have not learned to understand the psychological storms we encounter. Therefore, we are too often unable to protect ourselves, our families, and our communities from the psychic devastation storms leave behind. How can we as African Americans attempting to balance competing worldviews protect ourselves?

If we observe weather phenomenon, one can readily notice that sunshine and generally pleasant weather conditions prevail in an atmosphere of high pressure. If high pressure systems represent the Africentric worldview and value system, then we must surround ourselves with the ridges of high pressure. Nobles (1986) writes that "In the African way, ideas are the substance of behavior." Consequently, if our consciousness is culturally congruent, then our behavior should be focused on responding to our reality in ways which support, enhance, sustain, and actualize our individual and collective beings as African Americans. To assist us in this process, I would offer the following strategies.

Know Thy Self

It is not accidental that the prescription for mental health our ancestors left simply said "know thy self." Fundamentally, to know thy self means to recognize, understand, respect, appreciate, and love those characteristics which are uniquely African. It involves a reclamation of a consciousness and worldview that assists in the proper adaptation to ones reality. We must embrace our culture, study our history, and incorporate an Africentric value system into our life experiences. Be advised, however, that being Africentric is more than wearing a tee-shirt with a Black slogan on it, it's more than wearing a Malcolm X hat. It means placing African values at the center of our life experiences in any analysis we engage in. African values and value systems have been practiced and articulated by several male and female heroes, authors, families, communities, and others. Yet, I have observed that these important rules for living (values) and standards for conduct often go unrecognized because of our tendency to worship personalities of our heroes rather than understanding and operationalizing the principles by which they

66

conduct their lives. Indeed, it is the values of collective survival, harmony with the universe, respect for elders, self-sacrifice for the collective, truth, justice, righteousness, and connectedness to the divine Creator which has helped African people to not only survive nearly four-hundred years of oppression in this country, but survive through the ages.

Knowledge of self also speaks to the necessity of incorporating the principle of harmony into ones life. Achieving harmony requires a self-analysis, using the principle of congruence in asking ourselves: to what degree are our thoughts, feelings, intentions, and behaviors consistent with a culturally based (i.e. African) code of conduct? In other words, each of us must ask ourselves if we practice what we preach.

In some respects, knowing ones self requires that each African American understand and endorse (live by) the principle of consubstantiation. Nobles (1986) instructs us in his writings that in the African tradition, the notion of consubstantiation recognized that all elements of the universe were of the same substance. The recognition of the inner-connectedness between all people of African descent then allows for an understanding that our strength lies on our ability to recognize and utilize this collective strength for the betterment of our communities and, ultimately, ourselves.

It is the failure to incorporate this essential law of human functioning into our lives which helps to give rise to some of the self-destruction which our communities are witnessing. The escalation in the incidence of murder, drug abuse, robbery, sexual assault and child abuse discussed earlier clearly indicate that there is a crisis of consciousness. I believe that a cultural reorientation and adherence to principles like consubstantiation might reduce the destruction in our communities by allowing each of us to recognize that killing another brother or sister (or any human being) is not murder but really suicide; that personal drug use and abuse is detrimental to ones people; that sexual assault is actually a violation of self; and child abuse is in fact self-abuse.

Mastering Cultural Dispositions

In addition to knowing ones self, African American people must also understand and operationalize the principles of "self-determination" advocated by historical and contemporary African and African American leaders. Defining ones self, speaking for ones self, advocating for ones self, and supporting ones self at some level will help to create the high pressure systems necessary for psychological stability. Self-determination attitudes also help each of us to recognize that our degree of personal control over situational phenomenon will vary depending on the context and other individuals involved. In taking more control of our lives, and learning how to test what an environment will tolerate, we must learn to master the three African cultural dispositions outlined by Nobles (1986) in his book entitled *African Psychology*. They include:

Improvisation - where one seeks to spontaneously create, invent, or arrange a known experience into the unknown, thereby creating a new experience.

Transcendence - a quality, state, or ability to exceed, go beyond, or rise above the limits of an experience, condition, or situation. Meaning, "Sometimes, it just be like that," so we must accept it and move on.

Transformation - recognizing that a condition, quality, or nature of an experience has the potential to change into a different (and sometimes more positive) experience or element.

In essence, we must develop the capacity to improvise, transcend, or transform a negative experience or environmental situation into a more positive one. Whether your situation has you enduring a supervisor on the job who constantly harasses you, a professor or teacher who is racist in their approach, or even a prison or jail official who is oppressive in their treatment of you, each of you has the power to change and/or influence your situation. Even if the extent of your control is limited to two factors out of ten, at least attempt to control those two.

Differentiating Values And Skills

In focusing our attention on fortification, it is also important that African Americans begin to understand the fundamental difference between values and skills. Values are a "worth or importance that is assigned to something." Skills are "developed aptitudes or abilities at something;" it's the ability to use ones knowledge effectively in execution or performance. Values and skills are not necessarily synonymous. Too many of our youngsters however, assume that they are. Such a case was highlighted in the *Philadelphia Inquirer* newspaper on July 24, 1992. In that article, interviews were conducted with African American students who reported having to endure both self-imposed and other-imposed pressures of "acting White" if they achieved academic excellence (Barrington, 1992). Therefore, we must move beyond simplistic explanations which correlate excellence in reading, writing, mathematics, science, computer technology, and other endeavors with being White and selling out. Indeed, it was ancient Africa (Kemet) and not Europe who taught the world what it knows in almost every discipline. African American children and adults, students and workers can learn to execute the so-called "skills and technologies of the dominant culture," while simultaneously maintaining their own cultural values. We do not necessarily have to adopt Eurocentric oriented values, especially when they are to our detriment, just because we learn or utilize a particular skill. Conversely, we cannot afford to avoid acquiring a particular skill or competency that might assist us in advancing ourselves and our people simply because we associate that skill with being White. Our children must achieve scholastic excellence through reading and study, our adults must master new technologies of the 1990s, and our communities must confront illiteracy. Our challenge is to maintain our cultural integrity while learning the skills to navigate the pathways to productivity and success.

The Need for Cognitive Restructuring

Preparing for inevitable storms also requires that we as African American people develop a mental toughness. In essence, we must begin to mentally create positive and productive attitudes in ourselves. Because of the oppressive and non-affirming conditions we experience in American life, too many of us have developed attitudes which are destructive and counterproductive. These attitudes include:

a) worrying too much about what other people (especially Whites) think.

b) fear of failure such that we sometimes don't even try to confront a situation or problem.

c) low frustration tolerance, in that we become hypersensitive to the least little incident or inconvenience in our life.

d) tendency to blame others without recognizing our own responsibility for our life and life circumstances.

Consequently, we must begin to engage in cognitive restructuring, creating for ourselves the attitudes which will combat the low pressure systems (Eurocentric values, negative experiences with Whites) in our life experiences. The restructuring process requires a recognition that our emotional and behavioral responses to external events or situational phenomenon are not solely determined by these experiences. There is ample evidence to suggest that our responses are determined more by our belief system than by the events themselves (Ellis, 1973; Beck, et.al., 1979). In essence, the way you think influences how you feel and ultimately how you will respond in a given

71

situation. This strategy does not seek to ignore the very definite reality of oppression, discrimination, and racism. Rather, it seeks to re-establish some measure of control over those forces and situations to which we often yield all of our control and personal power. If we develop a belief system which is founded on powerlessness, then we are rendered helpless to change our own condition in America. Consequently, our only recourse is to plead assistance from those who neglect us in the first place. In my opinion, we should not be asking other people to do for us what we should be able to do for ourselves! Accordingly, since "ideas are the substance of behavior," counterproductive behaviors will never change unless we can replace negative belief systems with more positive ones.

Promote Collective Responsibility

Another strategy necessary for fortification requires that we as individuals who are part of a larger African American community must continue to operationalize the Africentric value of "I am because we are, and because we are, therefore I am." Historically, this Asanti proverb meant that an individual is only important to the degree that he or she contributes to the maintenance and survival of the tribe and/or the group. The proverb also helped each person to understand that individual needs for sustenance and support could be satisfied through interacting with and drawing upon the collective. Accordingly, there is a tremendous need for support group activities within the African American community. Men and women in our community should consider developing and maintaining forums for parental support, groups for professional networking and exchange (regardless of socioeconomic class), support groups for adolescents around manhood and womanhood training, support groups for students attending primary and secondary grades as well as institutions of higher education, and spiritual retreats which allow each of us to explore our own sense of spiritness, our relationship to the Creator, and our connectedness to the forces of nature.

In some cases, vehicles to provide support to community residents must be created. In other respects, no inventiveness is required; we only need to better utilize the mechanisms which are already in place.

One example of a tremendous resource in our communities are the Black fraternities and sororities. While credit must be given to those who work tirelessly at helping others, there are others whose efforts appear to be misdirected. Rather than midnight hazing sessions where pledges are verbally and physically abused under the guise of "promoting brotherhood or sisterhood" (as occurs in many undergraduate chapters), each pledge class should be given a task of working together to address larger community concerns like homelessness, healthcare information, education of children, sexual responsibility and AIDS education, voter registration, gang violence, and community policing, etc.

Submission To Divine Will

Fortifying ones psyche against the ravages of a psychic storm also requires the development of a positive self-concept. Indeed, that concept of self must contain a personal identity (self-portrait) which is rooted in ones Blackness, a reference group orientation which recognizes ones connection to and identification with other African people, a connectedness to an almighty supreme divine force, and a sense of esteem which radiates with pride and elation at ones cultural heritage. If we believe in the principle of "consubstantiation" (elements of the universe are of one substance), and we simultaneously recognize the existence of a higher force within the universe which is the source of all goodness and truth, then we must also recognize the necessity to develop a personal relationship with the Creator. In fact, Akbar (1984) reminds us that human potential is broadened or limited by ones conception of God. Consequently, developing a personal relationship with the divine Creator requires an awareness that there is a power or supreme force greater than yourself. An important distinction, however, should be made between the supreme "being" and a supreme or divine "force." Nobles (1986) reminds us that "Whatever is, is in the first place spirit." Meaning, our understanding of God cannot be confined to the search and glorification of a supreme being as manifest in the physical body of a man or a woman. Inevitably, such a quest leads to the dangerous practice of worshipping man-made divine images which do not reflect African people. Akbar (1984), and Blyden (1978) before him, cautions against such a practice because it forces African people to see God in an image of somebody other than ones self. Consequently, to the degree that we assign a superior status to images which do not reflect us, then at some level we must come to grips with the notion that we are inferior to the image and the people the image represents. Rather, our search for God is a quest for our own spiritness which gives enlightenment to our awareness of our potential to emulate God-like qualities of righteousness, truth, compassion, and love.

Submission to the will of the divine is a necessary prerequisite, for through our relationship with the Creator we come to realize our capacity for self-determination and our potential to achieve. Indeed, the ability to struggle in the face of adversity, to find truth where there is falsehood, to find strength when the soul (spirit) is weary, to find forgiveness when anger fills the heart, and to find comfort where chaos reigns is tied to accessing ones spiritness. This heightened state of awareness also helps us to understand that anchoring ones sense of self in a quest for and an attainment of material possessions is contrary to the will of God, and one's true spiritness.

Mental Health Assistance

Attempts to insulate our psyches from the ravages of the psychological storms do not have to be an exercise in rugged individualism. After all, we are a people who have endured through collective survival. An important and often underutilized resource could be an African American mental health professional (psychologist, therapist, counselor, etc.). Mental health personnel are professionally trained and credentialed to provide psychological services to various clientele. African American psychologists and counselors, especially those knowledgeable about Africentric therapeutic approaches and affiliated with the Association of Black Psychologists, are uniquely equipped to assist Black people with their mental struggles to balance competing worldviews.

In considering the use of mental health professionals, care should be exercised in avoiding the perception that utilization of a service is tantamount to a person being "crazy" or mentally ill. True enough, mental illness is a problem in our community. However, being distressed, anxious, hypersensitive or depressed about racist and oppressive conditions is, in fact, a "normal" response. When viewed in this context, mental health services are not designed to "fix" a client or patient; instead, they are an important source of support for people who are struggling to cope with life circumstances. Such support could be received during an individual therapy session, or in a structured (theme oriented) or unstructured support group. For example, members of your community might consider attending support groups for African American men, women, children, couples, etc.

Should consultation and/or therapy be sought from an African American mental health service provider, that experience is likely to result in the facilitation of a "culturally corrective experience" for that client. The therapeutic encounter(s) will involve an experience where the client would be assisted in: a) promoting thoughts, feelings and behaviors which affirm his/her humanity as a person of

African descent and,

b) purging from their mind, body and spirit those ideas, feelings and behaviors that prove destructive to their person and do nothing to support, enhance and promote a positive African self.

Consultation with and services by mental health professionals can be a very empowering experience for African American people. Despite the fact that traditional European American approaches to mental health assume the etiology (cause) of a person's psychological disturbance to be intrapsychic (within the mind of each individual), African American service providers recognize that personal distress is often caused by reactions to socially oppressive phenomenon. As a consequence, while psychological comfort can be given to assist with one's psychological adjustment, there is a simultaneous effort to impact the systemic forces which contribute to the distress. Learning how to impact systems outside of the individual can be empowering on two levels:

a) it helps a person to recognize that although they may be distressed, they are not "crazy" for feeling distressed and,

b) it helps a person to become less vulnerable to the social pathology which caused the distress in the first place.

Parenting Strategies

No set of strategies would be complete without reference to the offspring of African men and women. Undoubtedly, the most valuable resource of any community is its children. I believe strongly that parents must be present, actively involved, and willing to sacrifice personal comforts for the needs of their children. Without question, African American boys and girls will have their self-image assaulted by interacting with various institutions who do not support and affirm their humanity. The dilemma for parents and primary caregivers then is deciding both when to fortify and how to fortify our children. This dilemma we face today is not unlike that which many scholars and social scientists have articulated throughout the decades of the twentieth century. In his book entitled *The ABC of Color*, DuBois (1963) acknowledged that it was ill advised to introduce a child to race consciousness too early; but also dangerous to allow consciousness to develop and mature without proper guidance and direction. He wrote:

> "The day will arrive when mother must explain gently but clearly why the little girls next door do not want to play with niggers, and what the real cause of the teacher's unsympathetic attitude (is) . . . "

Questions of when to begin and how to accomplish the task of fortification are open to debate. Yet, there is some evidence which provides answers to both these questions. Research on self-esteem and the development of racial awareness in African Americans suggest that children's psyches are impacted as early as two and one-half to three years of age (Clark and Clark, 1947; Powell-Hopson and Hopson, 1990). At this early age, children's racial awareness often manifests itself in the form of comparisons to other children on skin tone, hair texture, eye color, etc. While this age is certainly too young to discuss the complexities of race relations or the dynamics of social oppression, it is an excellent opportunity for parents and others to provide positive affirmation and validation for those characteristics which make African American children unique. In fact, Drs. Powell-Hopson and Hopson (1990) in their text entitled *Different and Wonderful: Raising Black Children in a Race Conscious Society* speak to this issue as well by affirming that a child's inquisitiveness about his or her physical features provides parents with an excellent opportunity to praise their child's own physical attributes. Their text also provides some direction on "how to" by suggesting that important tools in combating low self-image and poor racial identity are talk (open acknowledgement of racial issues), positive modeling, and reinforcement of a child's cultural heritage (Blackness). Powell-Hopson and Hopson also suggest that parents need to understand and analyze their own biases, assumptions, values, and feelings before any assistance and proper guidance can be given to our children.

The Need For Self-Education

Our preparation for and fortification against the mental storms must also include self-initiated education. For too long, African people in America have been subjected to educational policies, practices and curricula which are often detrimental to our psyches. Unfortunately, we continue to be one of only a few ethnic groups or communities in America which does not systematically educate its children, youth and families. Consequently, we must do better. We cannot continue to depend solely on other people (especially White controlled educational institutions) to do for us what we undoubtedly can do for ourselves. Continuing to work within the confines of educational institutions (i.e. school boards, PTA's, etc.) to effect change is absolutely necessary. But ... it is far from sufficient. There is an answer to our frustration over unmotivated and uncaring teachers and irrelevant and unstimulating curricula: TEACH IT OURSELVES! Our minds are in need of some educational food which can only be provided by our community.

Each community or neighborhood should consider establishing a youth and adult book circle. Circles would meet regularly in neighbors' homes or other locations within the community where educational materials can be studied, discussed and exchanged. Community groups and even churches should also consider establishing Saturday schools where children and adults alike can come to study culturally specific curriculum outside of the normal school hours. Also, since an inordinately high percentage of our people (especially males) spend time incarcerated, attempts should be made to donate books and periodicals to jail and prison facilities for the purpose of exposing inmates to more self-knowledge. Of course, donations of materials should be coupled with donations of time where professionals and non-professionals alike volunteer their time to assist those who are incarcerated with their explorations of knowledge. Indeed, knowledge of ones culture and history is paramount to the fortification of our psyches.

CONCLUSION

———— · ◆ · ————

Among the many issues African Americans find themselves struggling with is the question of where to target our interventions. Given the racist and oppressive elements which characterize our lives in America, we can never afford to ignore the imperatives of self-determination, self-reliance, and self-protection. Indeed, the storms which characterize our mental struggles in this nation must be taken seriously and given appropriate priority. Thus, the primary focus of this manuscript has been to remain true to a theme of self-determination; high pressure systems do provide for clearer skies and summer days.

I would be negligent, however, if I concluded this manuscript without a comment on those forces which influence the low pressure dimensions of the psychic struggles most African Americans endure. The low pressure dimension of intolerance for anything or any person who is different is characteristic of a Eurocentric worldview and is a catalyst fueling the hurricane storm's development. Some might ask: why focus on the Eurocentric worldview at all? Well, I believe that if substantial progress in addressing issues of racism, etc. is to be realized, then European Americans (Whites) and other non-Blacks must begin to analyze their own thoughts, feelings, and behaviors. I have always found it interesting to note that most analyses of racism, oppression and discrimination are usually done from the perspective of the oppressed rather than the oppressor. When there is employment discrimination, we always ask how the victims feel. When there is a racist incident, we always ask how the victims feel. When there is the threat of social unrest, which existed in the wake of the trial of the police officers who beat Rodney Glenn King, we always want to ask how did Black people feel when the verdict was announced.

It is important to recognize that the substance and foundation for racism and intolerance cannot be revealed through an examination of the subjects of imposition (i.e. those who are oppressed). What I am suggesting is that the weather components which support low pressure systems are not composed of the attitudes of the victims of the storm. Rather, low pressure systems are supported by the ferocious winds of intolerance, the torrential rains of bigotry, and the massive clouds of ignorance, all of which emerge from the oppressor. Therefore, if during the calm after the storm, African American people are serious about preparing for the next one, then our analysis of data cannot be restricted to a survey of the devastation. Our focus must shed some light on the low pressure system itself, how it occurred, and how it impacts our climatic conditions.

The importance of this perspective is twofold. First, it allows those who are victimized by the hurricane storm to understand that the dissonance they feel is not totally rooted in themselves. Thus, the need for self-denegration lessens. Secondly, it encourages each person to stop surrounding themselves with low pressure systems and expecting sunny days. African people, you cannot seek validation from your oppressor!

I would also hope that the non-African folks (especially White people) who read this manuscript might accept these insights as an invitation to take a non-defensive look within themselves for some answers. Hurricane storms have a tendency to dissipate and lose their intensity once they reach land. Land masses symbolically represent attitudes of acceptance which help to change the social norms of intolerance. African Americans cannot be the only advocates for different normative standards; some of that advocacy must come from Whites and other non-Blacks themselves. White people cannot escape the label of racist or victimizer simply because they decline membership in a racist organization, or fail to engage in other racially derogatory behaviors themselves. If their vision is obstructed by the clouds of apathy and indifference, then they indirectly contribute to the storm by failing to calm the winds of intolerance or the rains of bigotry which emerge from their communities. Undoubtedly, African Americans cannot continue to fight that battle alone.

In closing, psychologically preparing ones self for the hurricane storm involves recognizing that storms (like rain, snow, clouds and sunshine) are unavoidable. Balancing competing Africentric and Eurocentric worldviews is a necessity. Living in an America which neither affirms nor validates your existence as an African American virtually guarantees that. However, be careful not to confuse needs for cultural and racial pride with ethnic hostility and hatred. Self-affirmation as an African American is not contingent upon denigrating White people or any other cultural group as a race of people. We must have a greater respect for humanity. We can, however, in our struggle for congruence stop seeking validation and approval from the oppressor. The eye of the hurricane that we seek is only an illusion, and it is not the safest place to be psychologically. Being out of the storm altogether seeking maximum congruence with ones cultural essence is ideal. Indeed, we must surround ourselves with the ridges of high pressure weather systems and create for ourselves the kind of climatic conditions which facilitate physical, mental, and spiritual growth.

Currently, the conditions in America indicate above average storm activity now and for the immediate future. Skies are cloudy with patches of blue sky and sunshine struggling to break through. The winds of change are blowing from the African continent at a high rate of speed. Barometric pressure is holding steady, but could rise or fall depending on the presence of high or low pressure systems in our lives. The extended weather forecast is hoping for partial clearing, followed by lots of sunshine, as high pressure systems dominate our weather patterns.

AFTERWORD

A RECIPE FOR CULTURAL GENOCIDE

What can be done to a race of people
to ensure that you **DOOM IT?**
You must first destroy its essential
component, the family **UNIT.**

INGREDIENTS

1) Add 1 cup of crushed psyche
   So that Brothas will **ASSUME** that
   Manhood is found in the **BEDROOM,**
   And Sistas will assess their **SELF-WORTH**
   By how many times they give **BIRTH.**

2) Add a teaspoon of inferiority so as to make
   These people feel like **CREATURES,**
   Then watch them go to great lengths
   To distort their strong African **FEATURES.**

3) Then stir thoroughly to rob
   These people of their **WEALTH,**
   Then for flavor add a dash
   Of the lack of knowledge of **SELF.**

4) Add a pound of lies
   To increase their **CONSTERNATION,**
   So that they never find out
   Who started **CIVILIZATION.**

5) One gram of **DECEIT**
   So that you can put the shackles
   On their minds
   Instead of their **FEET.**

6) Add 40 ounces of alcohol
   And 2 grams of **CRACK,**
   So that these people are
   Too inebriated to fight **BACK.**

7) Add 1 ounce of individualism and
   Simmer over the flame of **SELF-HATE,**
   And watch the Black on Black crime
   ESCALATE.

8) Add 1/2 pound of ignorance
   So that when it's time to **EAT,**
   These people will continue to poison themselves
   With pork chops, hamhocks, and **PIGS FEET.**

9) Measure two heaping tablespoons of capitalism
   So that when everyone is ready to revolt
   'Cause they can't **TAKE IT,**
   You let one through now
   Everyone thinks they can **MAKE IT.**

10) Slowly add the integration sauce
    With a pinch of **HOW TO'S,**
    And watch these people adopt
    Someone else's **VALUES.**

11) Pour into the saucepan of Amerikkkanism,
    So that even when these people are portrayed
    As miscreants, pimps, hustlers and **WHORES,**
    They'll continue to fight in your world,
    Vietnam and Persian Gulf **WARS.**

Then mix all the ingredients thoroughly and put into the oven of oppression for 400 years, and you're ready for a delicious helping of Cultural Genocide.

                                            Adisa Ajamu

REFERENCES

Akbar, N. (1981). Mental Disorders Among African Americans. *Black Books Bulletin.*

Akbar, N. (1984). *Chains and Images of Psychological Slavery.* Jersey City, NJ: Mind Productions.

Ames, R. (1950). Protest and Irony in Negro Folksong. *Social Science* (14), 193-213.

Azibo, D. (1989). Advances in Black/African Personality Theory. Unpublished Manuscript.

Baldwin, Joseph (1984). African Self-Consciousness and the Mental Health of African-Americans. *Journal of Black Studies,* 15, (2), 177-194.

Barrington, T. (1992). Fear of Acting White Blocks Some Black Students' Success. *The Philadelphia Inquirer,* July 24, 1992, pp. A-1 and A-13.

Clark, K. & Clark, M. (1947). Racial Identification and Preferences in Negro Children. *Readings in Social Psychology.* New York: Holt.

Cress-Welsing, F. (1991). *The Isis Papers: The Keys to the Colors.* Chicago: Third World Press.

Cross, W. (1971). The Negro to Black Conversion Experience: Toward a Psychology of Black Liberation. *Black World,* (20), 13-27.

DuBois, W.E.B. (1903). *The Souls of Black Folks.* New York: New American Library.

DuBois, W.E.B. (1963). *An ABC of Color.* New York: International Publishers.

Fanon, F. (1967). *Black Skin, White Masks.* New York: Grove Press.

Hopson, D.P. & Hopson, D.S. (1990). *Different and Wonderful: Raising Black Children in a Race Conscious Society.* New York: Prentice Hall.

Johnson, J. (1991). *Ebony Magazine* (August). Chicago: Johnson Publications.

Mbiti, J. (1970). *African Religions and Philosophies.* New York: Anchor Press.

Myers, L.J. (1988). *Understanding the Afrocentric World View.* Dubuque: Kendall/Hunt.

Nobles, W. (1986). *African Psychology: Toward Its Reclamation, Reassension, and Revitalization.* Oakland: Black Family Institute.

Nobles, W. (1980). African Philosophy: Foundations for Black Psychology. In R.L. Jones (2nd Ed.) *Black Psychology.* New York: Harper & Row.

Parham, T.A. (1989). Cycles of Psychological Nigrescence. *The Counseling Psychologist.* 17(2), 187-226.

Thomas, C. (1971). *Boys No More.* Beverly Hills: Glenco Press.

Whipple, A.B. (1982). *Planet Earth: Storm.* New York: Time Life Books.

White, J.L. & Parham, T.A. (1990). *The Psychology of Blacks: An African-American Perspective.* Englewood Cliffs, NJ: Prentice Hall.

White, J.L., Parham, W.D., & Parham, T.A. (1980). Black Psychology: The Afro-American Tradition as a Unifying Force for Traditional Psychology. In R.L. Jones (2nd Ed.) *Black Psychology.* New York: Harper & Row.

Williams, R.L. (1981). *The Collective Black Mind: An Afrocentric Theory of Black Personality.* St. Louis: Williams & Associates.